Self-Scoring

Personality

||||||||||||||||||||||||||||||||||||| Tests

Victor Serebriakoff

HONORARY INTERNATIONAL PRESIDENT, MENSA

Sterling Publishing Co., Inc.
New York

Published by Sterling Publishing Co., Inc.
387 Park Avenue South, New York, NY 10016

© 1968, 1988, 1996 by Victor Serebriakoff
Compilation © 1996 by Sterling Publishing Co., Inc.
This 1996 edition published by Sterling Publishing Co., Inc.,
by arrangement with Constable & Robinson Ltd.

Distributed in Canada by Sterling Publishing
c/o Canadian Manda Group, 165 Dufferin Street,
Toronto, Ontario, Canada M6K 3H6

Distributed in the United Kingdom by GMC Distribution Services,
Castle Place, 166 High Street, Lewes, East Sussex, England BN7 1XU

Distributed in Australia by Capricorn Link (Australia) Pty. Ltd.
P.O. Box 704, Windsor, NSW 2756, Australia

ISBN-13: 978-0-7607-0162-1
ISBN-10: 0-7607-0162-8

Printed in Canada
All rights reserved

40 39 38 37 36 35 34 33 32

For information about custom editions, special sales, premium and
corporate purchases, please contact Sterling Special Sales Department
at 800-805-5489 or specialsales@sterlingpub.com.

Disclaimer:
These tests are not meant to replace a professional examination. The accepted view is
that the only valid test is an individual test administered by a qualified professional.

PERSONALITY FACTORS

Everyone has different behavior patterns that vary from time to time with mood changes, fits of temper, laughter, fear, or joy. Behind these emotional changes we are aware of deeper patterns and more permanent tendencies, comprising what is called personality, that make it possible for us to classify people in a number of other ways.

In developing a science of the mind, psychometricians were confronted with a large number of supposedly distinct personality types. In the hope of simplifying matters (which is *always* the job of the scientist), they worked on the assumption that there may in fact be only a few basic personality types and that from each basic type there derives a great many variations on a theme. They consulted an arsenal of statistical techniques to find out to what extent each personality type relates to another. If they found a strong relation, they assumed that there must be a common factor operating underneath. They discovered that personality types could be fitted into clusters or clumps that are interrelated.

It is a characteristic of the human mind that in order to deal with new information it must first classify it. In this manner, scientists eventually agree on the most useful method of classification for a new science, and from that framework the science grows. But in the early days of any scientific inquiry, many different classification methods are tried out before the most effective and accurate one is found. The truth or accuracy of any system of classification depends on the questions we ask. Some questions elicit more useful information than others. This booklet contains the most accepted method of classification and the most revealing questions available at this time.

In today's world more than ever, demands are made on people to fit highly specified roles. We can, via trial and error, find the roles that best suit us. But if we are wise, we will pay attention to psychometrics, which, without prejudice, can help us know ourselves better. Only when we have taken the measure of our personalities can we get the most out of them.

—*Victor Serebriakoff*
1996

Take all four tests first, then use the key on pages 19–23 to interpret your scores.

PERSONALITY FACTOR 1

How to take the test
There are no right or wrong answers to the questions.

Answer the questions quickly and spontaneously. It is your emotional reaction that is being checked, not your thought processes, so do not worry about possible illogicalities. Answer impulsively and quickly.

Circle your answer as A or B.

Test begins here

(1)	Would you prefer to be a research scientist in a lab (A) or a senator (B)?	A or B
(2)	Do you feel that many professions or occupations that are considered honest do more harm to the country (A) than good (B)?	A or B
(3)	Which is more important in a literary critic, to be tolerant and encouraging (A) or discriminating (B)?	A or B
(4)	If you had the choice of working as a receptionist (B) or being your own boss (A), which would you choose?	A or B
(5)	Should a doctor put personal feelings aside while determining the treatment of patients (A), or should feelings be one of his or her main guides (B)?	A or B
(6)	Do you find it easy (B) or hard (A) to adapt your behavior according to the company you are in?	A or B
(7)	While on vacation do you prefer to spend most of your time reading (A) or meeting people (B)?	A or B
(8)	Would being a hermit come easily (A) or with difficulty to you (B)?	A or B
(9)	Would you prefer to marry a person who is (A) a thoughtful companion or (B) very sociable?	A or B
(10)	Are most people likely (B) or unlikely (A) to be trustworthy?	A or B
(11)	Do you like (A) or dislike (B) throwing parties?	A or B
(12)	Would you prefer to be a traveling salesperson (B) or a bookkeeper in an office (A)?	A or B

(13)   Would you describe yourself as an optimist (B) or a pessimist (A)?   A or B

(14)   Would you prefer to be a high civil servant (A) or a senator (B)?   A or B

(15)   Do you usually enjoy (B) or not enjoy (A) big, noisy parties?   A or B

(16)   Would you find it difficult (A) or easy (B) to make a public speech?   A or B

(17)   In a dramatic production, would you be happier working backstage (A) or as a leading actor (B)?   A or B

(18)   Are you very quick (B) or rather slow (A) at making a witty reply in most conversations?   A or B

(19)   Are you usually quick (B) or slow (A) at making new friends in a new situation?   A or B

(20)   Would you describe yourself as being full of energy (B) or lethargic (A)?   A or B

Now count your A's and B's. Write down your score.

Total score: A_____ B _____

Now go on to the next test. Do not look at the key yet.

PERSONALITY FACTOR 2

How to take the test
Once again you should be in a decisive frame of mind and go through the questions quickly. The test should be completed in about ten minutes, but it is of no great significance if you take more or less time.

Test begins here

(1)   As far as you know, have you ever (A) or never (B) walked in your sleep?   A or B

(2)   Have you (A) or have you not (B) taken more sick days from work than most people?   A or B

(3)   Do you (A) or do you not (B) feel confused if you are interrupted while working?   A or B

(4)   Do you (A) or do you not (B) exercise hard every day?   A or B

(5)   The last time you began to learn a new skill, did you (B) or did you not
       (A) feel confident?   A or B

(6)   Have you (A) or have you not (B) felt aggravated about trivial
       irritations?   A or B

(7)   Have you ever (A) or have you never (B) agonized for hours after being in
       a situation that felt humiliating to you?   A or B

(8)   Would many people regard you as a sensitive person (A) or not (B)?   A or B

(9)   Do you (B) or do you not (A) usually fall asleep easily and sleep well?   A or B

(10)   Would many people consider you shy (A) or not (B)?   A or B

(11)   Do you (A) or do you not (B) feel much disturbed if a friend fails to
       greet you?   A or B

(12)   Do you (A) or do you not (B) sometimes feel happy or sad without any
       real cause?   A or B

(13)   Do you (A) or do you not (B) often find yourself daydreaming when
       you should be working?   A or B

(14)   Can you (A) or can you not (B) remember having any nightmares in
       the last five years?   A or B

(15)   Do you (A) or do you not (B) have fear of heights or elevators or
       tunnels or going outside?   A or B

(16)   Do you (B) or do you not (A) usually behave calmly and efficiently in
       an emergency?   A or B

(17)   Do you (A) or do you not (B) believe yourself to be an emotional
       person in many everyday life situations?   A or B

(18)   Do you (A) or do you not (B) frequently worry about your health?   A or B

(19)   Can you (A) or can you not (B) remember annoying someone in the
       last year?   A or B

(20)   Do you (A) or do you not (B) perspire a lot without having exercised?   A or B

(21)   Can you (A) or can you not (B) remember your mind going blank in the middle of doing a job within the last five years?   A or B

(22)   Have you (A) or have you not (B) met as many as three people that you have decided were definitely unfriendly toward you within the last year?   A or B

(23)   Have you ever (A) or have you never (B) been short of breath when you are not exercising?   A or B

(24)   Are you generally tolerant of other people's idiosyncracies (B) or not (A)?   A or B

(25)   Are there (A) or are there not (B) any everyday situations in which you feel very self-conscious?   A or B

(26)   Do you often feel unhappy (A) or not (B)?   A or B

(27)   Have you (A) or have you not (B) suffered from diarrhea more than once in the last two years?   A or B

(28)   Are you usually self-confident (B) or not (A)?   A or B

(29)   Do you (A) or do you not (B) have any reason to believe that you cannot manage the situations of life as easily as most people?   A or B

(30)   Do you (A) or do you not (B) use aspirin, codeine, sedatives, pep pills, sleeping pills, or other drugs more than once a month?   A or B

Now count your A's and B's and write down your score.

Total score: A____   B ____

Now go on to the next test. Do not look at the key yet.

PERSONALITY FACTOR 3

Test
begins
here

How to take the test

Use the printed lines in each of the squares as a basis for fifteen original drawings of recognizable images. Draw clearly but quickly. Do not bother with details. Make as many *different* drawings as possible in five minutes.

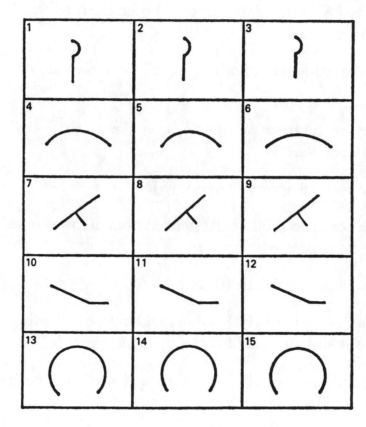

Now go on to the next test. Do not look at the key yet.

PERSONALITY FACTOR 4

How to take the test

Answer the questions quickly and without reflection; give your immediate reaction to the question.

If your answer is yes, then circle the letter after the word Yes; if it is no, circle the letter after the word No. If you are in doubt or hesitant, circle the question mark (?).

Test begins here

(1)	Do you prefer your life to be full of changes?	Yes (Y) (?) No (X)
(2)	Are you an ambitious person?	Yes (Y) (?) No (X)
(3)	"Politicians are generally sincere and do their best for the country." Do you think this is so?	Yes (X) (?) No (Y)
(4)	When doing things, do you choose to hide from others the motives behind them?	Yes (Y) (?) No (X)
(5)	Rather than dream of success, do you work hard to achieve it?	Yes (Y) (?) No (X)
(6)	Would you rather be alive and a coward than dead and a hero?	Yes (Y) (?) No (X)
(7)	Would you be more upset by the loss of material things than by hearing of a friend's illness?	Yes (X) (?) No (Y)
(8)	Do you get your way without regard for other people's feelings?	Yes (Y) (?) No (X)
(9)	Do you feel vengeful if a person hurts you?	Yes (Y) (?) No (X)
(10)	Do you worry about work while on vacation?	Yes (Y) (?) No (X)
(11)	Do you compare your performance with that of other colleagues?	Yes (Y) (?) No (X)
(12)	When you get into a heated discussion, do you find it difficult to calm down and stop?	Yes (Y) (?) No (X)
(13)	Are romantic stories among your reading material?	Yes (X) (?) No (Y)
(14)	Do you take shortcuts in order to work fast?	Yes (Y) (?) No (X)

(15)   Do you set your goals too low because you are afraid of
        failure?   Yes (X) (?) No (Y)

(16)   If given the chance, would you like to witness an
        execution?   Yes (Y) (?) No (X)

(17)   Are you cool-minded in dealing with people?   Yes (Y) (?) No (X)

(18)   Do you prepare thoroughly for tests?   Yes (Y) (?) No (X)

(19)   Do you sometimes tell white lies?   Yes (Y) (?) No (X)

(20)   Do you enjoy dancing?   Yes (X) (?) No (Y)

(21)   If somebody sat in front of you and obstructed your view
        with a hat, would you ask him or her to remove it?   Yes (Y) (?) No (X)

(22)   Would you enjoy traveling at 150 mph in a race car?   Yes (Y) (?) No (X)

(23)   Did you prefer English literature over science at school?   Yes (Y) (?) No (X)

(24)   Do you think that most politicians are dishonest?   Yes (Y) (?) No (X)

(25)   Do you hold stronger opinions than most people?   Yes (X) (?) No (Y)

(26)   Do you flatter people so that you can improve your status
        in life?   Yes (Y) (?) No (X)

(27)   Did you always do as you were told when you were young?   Yes (X) (?) No (Y)

(28)   Did you enjoy playing with guns as a child?   Yes (Y) (?) No (X)

(29)   Would you rather be a dentist than a dress designer?   Yes (Y) (?) No (X)

(30)   Do you place achievement among the most important
        things in life?   Yes (Y) (?) No (X)

(31)   Do you work hard to get ahead?   Yes (Y) (?) No (X)

(32)   Do you stand on an escalator rather than walk on it?   Yes (X) (?) No (Y)

(33)   Would you feel it best not to respond if a person is rude
        to you?   Yes (Y) (?) No (X)

(34) Do you prefer climates of even temperature? Yes (X) (?) No (Y)

(35) Would you ask someone to stop smoking in your presence? Yes (Y) (?) No (X)

(36) Do you like watching aggressive sports on television? Yes (Y) (?) No (X)

(37) Is love more important than success? Yes (Y) (?) No (X)

(38) If you were standing in line, would you react if a person went to the front out of turn? Yes (Y) (?) No (X)

(39) Have you ever felt the urge to kill someone? Yes (Y) (?) No (X)

(40) If you were on a committee, would you be in charge? Yes (Y) (?) No (X)

(41) If you disapproved of a friend's behavior, would you make him or her aware of your feelings? Yes (X) (?) No (Y)

(42) Would you take any drugs that cause hallucinations? Yes (Y) (?) No (X)

(43) Do you try new innovations rather than stick to tested methods? Yes (Y) (?) No (X)

(44) Do you get so angry with people that you shout at them? Yes (Y) (?) No (X)

(45) Do you make a creative contribution to society? Yes (Y) (?) No (X)

(46) Do you enjoy what you do at work? Yes (X) (?) No (Y)

(47) Do you see the world in gray rather than black and white? Yes (X) (?) No (Y)

(48) Do you hesitate to ask strangers questions? Yes (X) (?) No (Y)

(49) Do you crave excitement? Yes (Y) (?) No (X)

(50) Do you believe that there are better reasons for marriage than love? Yes (Y) (?) No (X)

(51) Would you travel to a different part of the world to live? Yes (X) (?) No (Y)

(52) Do you socialize with people who can help you? Yes (Y) (?) No (X)

(53) Would you consider it too dangerous to go mountain climbing? Yes (X) (?) No (Y)

(54)   Do you win people over by telling them what they want to
         hear?   Yes (Y) (?) No (X)

(55)   Do you prefer not to sit in a conspicuous place in a
         lecture room?   Yes (X) (?) No (Y)

(56)   Do you know the difference between right and wrong?   Yes (Y) (?) No (X)

(57)   Do you prefer ordinary sex?   Yes (X) (?) No (Y)

(58)   Do you try to shock people?   Yes (Y) (?) No (X)

(59)   Do you believe in "every man for himself"?   Yes (Y) (?) No (X)

(60)   Do you agree that "fools and their money are soon parted"?   Yes (Y) (?) No (X)

(61)   Do you like buying things?   Yes (X) (?) No (Y)

(62)   Does other people's ignorance appall you?   Yes (Y) (?) No (X)

(63)   Do you take care of things today rather than leave them
         until tomorrow?   Yes (Y) (?) No (X)

(64)   Would you like to learn to be a pilot?   Yes (Y) (?) No (X)

(65)   Do you have a burning ambition to be of great impor-
         tance in the community?   Yes (X) (?) No (Y)

(66)   Do you watch pornographic videos?   Yes (Y) (?) No (X)

(67)   Do you dislike foreigners?   Yes (X) (?) No (Y)

(68)   When reading newspaper reports, do you get annoyed at
         what some politicians say?   Yes (X) (?) No (Y)

(69)   Do you advocate force where necessary?   Yes (X) (?) No (Y)

(70)   Do you draw in children's drawing books?   Yes (X) (?) No (Y)

(71)   Do you enjoy physical activity of a rough nature?   Yes (Y) (?) No (X)

(72)   Do you feel sorry for injured birds?   Yes (X) (?) No (Y)

(73)   When you are working, can you listen to people at the
         same time?   Yes (Y) (?) No (X)

(74)   Are you inclined to be lazy?   Yes (X) (?) No (Y)

(75)   Have you ever modeled yourself on somebody?   Yes (Y) (?) No (X)

(76)   Do you take excessive pride in your work?   Yes (Y) (?) No (X)

(77)   Do you avoid disaster scenes on television?   Yes (X) (?) No (Y)

(78)   Can you persuade people?   Yes (Y) (?) No (X)

(79)   Are you a leader in a group of people?   Yes (Y) (?) No (X)

(80)   Do you give the real reason when asking somebody to do
       something for you?   Yes (X) (?) No (Y)

(81)   Do you think that most people are good?   Yes (X) (?) No (Y)

(82)   Are you a natural organizer?   Yes (Y) (?) No (X)

(83)   Do you think before you speak?   Yes (Y) (?) No (X)

(84)   Do you dislike snakes?   Yes (X) (?) No (Y)

(85)   Do you sometimes have cruel fantasies?   Yes (Y) (?) No (X)

(86)   Do you believe that people with extreme political views
       should inflict their opinions on others?   Yes (X) (?) No (Y)

(87)   Do you believe that all religions are basically the same? Yes (Y) (?) No (X)

(88)   Is it essential that you succeed in your life?   Yes (Y) (?) No (X)

(89)   Do you concentrate on one great cause?   Yes (Y) (?) No (X)

(90)   Do you try to compromise with opponents?   Yes (Y) (?) No (X)

(91)   Do you get annoyed when people do not admit that they
       are wrong?   Yes (Y) (?) No (X)

(92)   Do you always take damaged goods back for exchange?   Yes (Y) (?) No (X)

(93)   Are you more interested in science than personal
       relationships?   Yes (Y) (?) No (X)

(94)   Do you like being the center of attention?   Yes (Y) (?) No (X)

(95)   Do you fear boredom?   Yes (Y) (?) No (X)

(96)   Are you aware of the beauty surrounding you?   Yes (Y) (?) No (X)

(97)	Would you like to be an astronaut?	Yes (Y) (?) No (X)
(98)	Do you believe that playing is more important than winning?	Yes (X) (?) No (Y)
(99)	Do you criticize people who are conceited?	Yes (Y) (?) No (X)
(100)	Would you go to a wife-swapping party?	Yes (Y) (?) No (X)
(101)	Are you often furious with other people?	Yes (Y) (?) No (X)
(102)	Are you drawn to unfortunate people?	Yes (X) (?) No (Y)
(103)	Do you horse around at the swimming pool?	Yes (Y) (?) No (X)
(104)	Are you scared of the dark?	Yes (X) (?) No (Y)
(105)	Do you state your opinions with vehemence?	Yes (Y) (?) No (X)
(106)	Do you hurt other people in order to get what you want?	Yes (Y) (?) No (X)
(107)	Do you think that pacifists are cowards?	Yes (X) (?) No (Y)
(108)	Do you dislike spicy food?	Yes (X) (?) No (Y)
(109)	Are you scared of spiders and worms?	Yes (X) (?) No (Y)
(110)	Do you believe it is *always* best to be honest?	Yes (X) (?) No (Y)
(111)	Do you try to understand the other person's point of view in a conflict?	Yes (X) (?) No (Y)
(112)	Does it annoy you when experts are proved wrong?	Yes (Y) (?) No (X)
(113)	Would you like to be a lion hunter?	Yes (Y) (?) No (X)
(114)	Do you disregard other people's feelings?	Yes (Y) (?) No (X)
(115)	Are you often unsure about whom to vote for?	Yes (X) (?) No (Y)
(116)	Are you easily startled?	Yes (X) (?) No (Y)
(117)	Would you like to appear on television?	Yes (Y) (?) No (X)
(118)	Do you like to pick up furry animals?	Yes (X) (?) No (Y)
(119)	Do you like to take orders?	Yes (X) (?) No (Y)
(120)	Does your intuition tell you whether a person is trustworthy?	Yes (X) (?) No (Y)

(121)   Are you easily bored?   Yes (Y) (?) No (X)

(122)   Do you argue when you know you are wrong?   Yes (Y) (?) No (X)

(123)   Would you help somebody in need?   Yes (X) (?) No (Y)

(124)   Do you like practical jokes?   Yes (X) (?) No (Y)

(125)   Are you satisfied with your salary?   Yes (X) (?) No (Y)

(126)   Are you slow to trust people?   Yes (Y) (?) No (X)

(127)   Are you scared of people in authority?   Yes (X) (?) No (Y)

(128)   Are you emotional when watching a film?   Yes (X) (?) No (Y)

(129)   Do you prefer Mozart to Wagner?   Yes (X) (?) No (Y)

(130)   Do you obey signs?   Yes (X) (?) No (Y)

(131)   Do you think about falling in love?   Yes (X) (?) No (Y)

(132)   Do you believe that we can learn from other cultures?   Yes (X) (?) No (Y)

(133)   Do you find it hard to say no to a salesman?   Yes (X) (?) No (Y)

(134)   Do you get excited when talking about your work?   Yes (X) (?) No (Y)

(135)   Can you make up excuses easily?   Yes (Y) (?) No (X)

(136)   Do you like a peaceful life?   Yes (X) (?) No (Y)

(137)   Do you take risks?   Yes (Y) (?) No (X)

(138)   Do you break dishes when annoyed?   Yes (X) (?) No (Y)

(139)   Are you jealous of other people's success?   Yes (Y) (?) No (X)

(140)   Do you engage in political protest?   Yes (X) (?) No (Y)

(141)   Do you read science fiction?   Yes (Y) (?) No (X)

(142)   Do you blame someone else when things go wrong?   Yes (Y) (?) No (X)

(143)   Do you stay in the background at parties?   Yes (X) (?) No (Y)

(144)   Do you try to convert others to your religion?   Yes (Y) (?) No (X)

(145)   Does your work keep you awake at night because you find
        it so interesting?   Yes (Y) (?) No (X)

(146)   Does the sight of blood make you feel queasy?   Yes (Y)   (?)   No (X)

(147)   Do you scold people who offend you?   Yes (Y)   (?)   No (X)

(148)   Do you mix with people who are unpredictable and nonconformist?   Yes (Y)   (?)   No (X)

(149)   Do you avoid thrilling rides at the carnival?   Yes (X)   (?)   No (Y)

(150)   Would you fight for your rights rather than give them up without a struggle?   Yes (Y)   (?)   No (X)

(151)   Do you always tell the truth?   Yes (X)   (?)   No (Y)

(152)   Do you stop yourself from being lazy?   Yes (Y)   (?)   No (X)

(153)   Are you too amenable at work?   Yes (X)   (?)   No (Y)

(154)   Do you frequently grind your teeth?   Yes (Y)   (?)   No (X)

(155)   Do you sometimes question your own actions?   Yes (X)   (?)   No (Y)

(156)   If you are right, do you argue?   Yes (Y)   (?)   No (X)

(157)   Does your sympathy lie with the underdog?   Yes (X)   (?)   No (Y)

(158)   Do you cry sometimes?   Yes (X)   (?)   No (Y)

(159)   Are you regarded as too good-natured?   Yes (X)   (?)   No (Y)

(160)   Do you like violent scenes in the movies or on television?   Yes (Y)   (?)   No (X)

(161)   Do you like strong debates?   Yes (Y)   (?)   No (X)

(162)   Did you avoid fighting when you were young?   Yes (X)   (?)   No (Y)

(163)   Are you a relentless worker?   Yes (Y)   (?)   No (X)

(164)   Are you sarcastic?   Yes (Y)   (?)   No (X)

(165)   Do you like shooting galleries?   Yes (Y)   (?)   No (X)

(166)   Do you relax on vacation and forget about work?   Yes (X)   (?)   No (Y)

(167)   Do you enjoy horror films?   Yes (Y)   (?)   No (X)

(168)   In an argument, are you firm and forthright?   Yes (Y)   (?)   No (X)

(169)   Are you mechanically minded?   Yes (Y) (?) No (X)

(170)   Do you often change your mind?   Yes (X) (?) No (Y)

(171)   Do you dislike vulgar jokes?   Yes (X) (?) No (Y)

(172)   Are you patient?   Yes (X) (?) No (Y)

(173)   Do you get closely involved with people?   Yes (X) (?) No (Y)

(174)   Are you mild-tempered?   Yes (X) (?) No (Y)

(175)   Would it be beneficial if we all shared the same ideas and
          opinions?   Yes (Y) (?) No (X)

(176)   Do you like war stories?   Yes (Y) (?) No (X)

(177)   Do you sometimes go through the whole day without
          achieving anything?   Yes (X) (?) No (Y)

(178)   Do you watch fight scenes on television?   Yes (Y) (?) No (X)

(179)   Are you good at bluffing?   Yes (Y) (?) No (X)

(180)   Are you forgiving to people who have wronged you? Yes (X) (?) No (Y)

(181)   Do you always stick to your decision?   Yes (Y) (?) No (X)

(182)   Are you happy with our government?   Yes (X) (?) No (Y)

(183)   Do you wish to "better yourself"?   Yes (Y) (?) No (X)

(184)   Do you believe that a good teacher is one who makes you
          think, rather than one who only teaches?   Yes (X) (?) No (Y)

(185)   Do you enjoy watching rough sports?   Yes (Y) (?) No (X)

(186)   Is your way of tackling problems better than other people's? Yes (Y) (?) No (X)

(187)   Do you complain to the management if the service is bad
          in a restaurant?   Yes (X) (?) No (Y)

(188)   Do you pay attention to other people's viewpoints? Yes (Y) (?) No (X)

(189)   Do you like autobiographies?   Yes (Y) (?) No (X)

(190)   Do you put your interests first?   Yes (Y) (?) No (X)

(191)   Would you hesitate before shooting a burglar?   Yes (X)   (?)   No (Y)

(192)   Do you make friends with people because they can help you?   Yes (Y)   (?)   No (X)

(193)   Do you believe there is some truth in everybody's views?   Yes (Y)   (?)   No (X)

(194)   Do you like bustle around you?   Yes (Y)   (?)   No (X)

(195)   Do you wish you were more assertive?   Yes (X)   (?)   No (Y)

(196)   Are you sometimes irritable?   Yes (X)   (?)   No (Y)

(197)   Do you like quiet paintings rather than vivid paintings?   Yes (X)   (?)   No (Y)

(198)   Do you lose your temper less often than the average person?   Yes (X)   (?)   No (Y)

(199)   Do you agree rather than argue?   Yes (X)   (?)   No (Y)

(200)   When you are angry, do you stamp your feet?   Yes (Y)   (?)   No (X)

(201)   Do underwater sports interest you?   Yes (Y)   (?)   No (X)

(202)   Do you repeat yourself?   Yes (Y)   (?)   No (X)

(203)   Do you enjoy helping other people?   Yes (X)   (?)   No (Y)

(204)   Would you like to try parachute jumping?   Yes (Y)   (?)   No (X)

(205)   Are you belligerent?   Yes (Y)   (?)   No (X)

(206)   Would you take part in an orgy?   Yes (Y)   (?)   No (X)

(207)   Do you socialize with people of other religions?   Yes (X)   (?)   No (Y)

(208)   Do you stand up for yourself?   Yes (Y)   (?)   No (X)

(209)   Do you sing in a choir?   Yes (X)   (?)   No (Y)

(210)   Do you tend to get pushed around?   Yes (X)   (?)   No (Y)

Now count the Y's, the ?'s, and the X's you have circled.

Total score: Y____   ?____   X____

KEY TO INTERPRETING YOUR SCORES

Finished? Refer back to each of the four personality tests for your "Total score." Now compare each of the scores to its accompanying interpretation. Personality Factor 3 will have its own separate means of measurement.

Personality Factor 1: Extroversion

The extrovert (one who is directed outward) and the introvert (directed inward) represent the extremes of human sociability. Most people are somewhere in between. People will be more extroverted on some occasions and less on others, but usually tend to remain about the same. Over the long term, most people show a slight trend toward extroversion.

The extrovert is an outward-looking, friendly, and uninhibited person. Extroverts enjoy company, feel comfortable in a group, and tend to form many friendships of varying depth. Introverts often prefer to be alone with their thoughts and tend to form one or a few profound attachments. They are the type who like to keep their feelings to themselves. Neither type of personality is good or bad, although it is probably preferable to have a balance of extrovert and introvert tendencies.

The more A's you circled, the more introverted you are. 15 or so would make you definitely introverted, and 20 very much so. 15 B's make you an extrovert, and 20, a bouncing extrovert.

Introversion/Extroversion
(Judged by your results on the Personality Factor 1 Test)

No. of A's	Character	No. of A's	Character
20	Extremely introverted	8/7	A shade extroverted
19	Very introverted	6/5	Slightly extroverted
18	Quite introverted	4/3	Somewhat extroverted
17/16	Somewhat introverted	2	Quite extroverted
15/14	Slightly introverted	1	Very extroverted
13/12	A shade introverted	0	Extremely extroverted
11/10/9	Average		

Personality Factor 2: Emotional Stability

The answers you give decide whether you are emotionally sensitive or impervious. Those with 20 or so B's are very self-possessed, never seem to get upset, are equable and balanced, and probably go through life without the ups and downs of the more sensitive type of person. Those with a score of more than 20 A's are emotional and suggestible, and probably feel the mental strains of life more than most. On the other hand, those with 22 or so B's are a bit phlegmatic and might try to arrange life so as to present some challenge to their placidity.

Stability

(Judged by your results on the Personality Factor 2 Test)

No. of B's	Character
30/29	Unshakable
28/27	Imperturbable
26/25	Unflappable
24/23	Calm
22/21	Balanced
20/19/18	Steady
17/16/15/14	Average
13/12/11	Sympathetic
10/9	Suggestible
8/7	Emotional
6/5	Sensitive
4/3	Oversensitive
2/1	Nervous
0	Neurotic

As with most personality factors but emphatically not with intelligence, it is the intermediate scores that are the best.

Both tendencies have advantages in certain social roles. We would not want our lover to be phlegmatic and insensitive. But we might prefer our lawyer to be calm enough not to burst into tears at a harsh word from the opposing counsel.

Personality Factor 3: Creativity

Give yourself one point for each recognizable drawing, provided it does not fall into the same category as any other drawing on the same sheet. You are penalized for using the same idea twice. For instance, only one human face is allowed, and a second one gets no marks unless it is a detail in the drawing and not the whole subject. If you are "creative" you will tend to variety naturally, even if you are not instructed.

There is no right answer to a creativity test; there is an infinite number of possible answers and they are all equally right provided they are imaginative and not copied, and provided they take into account all the features of the problem situation. In these problems you are asked to utilize the whole of the diagram given. If any part of the diagram is not used in your drawing, then you do not get the point. It is, of course, best to get a friend to assess your work after getting him or her to read the instructions carefully.

Creativity

(Judged by your results on the Personality Factor 3 Test)

No. of complete, original, unrepetitive drawings	Character
1	Uncreative
2	
3	
4	
5	
6	
7/8	Average
9	
10	
11	
12	
13	
14	
15	Very creative

If the concept of "intelligence" as a human personality factor is disputed, then the concept of "creativity" is barely established. Creativity has a relatively thin background scientifically, but a great fuss has been made about a little body of actual experimental work.

I shall try to consider creativity apart from its political undertones and overtones. Going by the evidence that is most convincing to me and least convincing to others—that is, my own experience—I feel that it is possible to distinguish people by some criterion that could be reasonably called creativity. Some people are more adept at combining and recombining ideas into original forms. The difference appears to be in the field of hypothesis-making. If problem-solving is often a matter of trial and error, of adjusting and modifying conceptual frameworks until one with a relatively good fit is found, then "creatives" seem to me to be those who are more prolific at generating hypotheses. Their ability to judge the hypotheses when formed and to reject the inadequate would be associated with pure intelligence. But their ability to produce sheer quantity of theories to be tested, though associated with intelligence, is not due to intelligence itself.

Like other psychometric tests, creativity tests must be judged by whether they can be validated statistically.

Personality Factor 4: Strong-Mindedness

Count two points for each circled (Y) and one point for each circled (?). Do not bother with the circled X's. Find your total in the following table, which shows a continuum of Factor 4 scores ranging from over 400 down to 0. You can regard these as points on a scale where a high score means strong-mindedness. High scores point to an emphatic, assertive, tough-talking, manipulative, dogmatic, stimulus-hungry, adventurous personality. Low scores indicate a weak will or submissiveness. Somewhere in between seems best, and that is where most people are. Both "winners" and "losers" will tend to come from the high-scoring end (because high Factor 4 people are risk-takers), but in peaceful times long-term survivors will tend to be low scorers. We know the "Win or bust" attitude and the "Don't get involved" attitude. The first would have high scores, the second low ones on this scale.

Strong-Mindedness

(Judged by your results on the Personality Factor 4 Test)

No. of Points	Character
Over 400	Very aggressive, inflexible, bossy
350–400	Strong-willed, confrontational
300–350	Determined, authoritative
250–300	Assertive, managerial
200–250	A balanced personality, diplomatic
150–200	Shy, warm-hearted
100–150	Sympathetic, caring, but weak-willed
50–100	Unambitious, eager to please
Below 50	Very timid, easily dominated

Personality Factor 4 is the general attitude toward life and other people. It could be called the competitive versus cooperative approach or the self-centered versus caring attitude.

Social life involves a balance between competition and cooperation. A sense of competition between people brings out effort, keenness, and adventurousness. On the other hand, without mutual consideration, social interactions cannot survive. A balance is essential.

We are dealing with two basic elements in human nature. Those who are very high in Factor 4 are likely to be bossy, tough-minded, and competitive. They will want to be respected more than they will want to be loved.

Those who score lower are likely to be compassionate, caring, impressionable, and even suggestible. They may prefer subordinate roles, and prefer to be loved rather than feared.

The test in this booklet is based on several tests, each of which measures factors that relate to general attitude. Very high scorers will be vengeful and even aggressive. High scorers will be assertive, have a strong personality, be ambitious, energetic, and eager to raise their status. They will tend to be rigid, inflexible, and unyielding in opinion and policy. They will have what is called "stimulus hunger"; they will enjoy challenge, adventure, and risk-taking.

How about low scorers? The few very low scorers will be timid, humble, and low on initiative. They will be uncompetitive and unambitious, pleasant, and self-effacing. They will be trusting, unselfish, caring, good-hearted, and, at the extreme, gullible. At medium-low scores they will be flexible and cooperative. More so than high scorers, they will be ready for accommodation and compromise.

Perhaps the most important result of taking a personality test is not your score but the discovery of where your strengths and weaknesses are. This knowledge may help you to tailor your lifestyle to the needs of your personality—rather than strain yourself in order to meet the demands of a life that does not make you happy.